I0752806

Nov, '80
WEISBRODT

IDYLS AND LYRICS OF THE OHIO VALLEY,

BY

JOHN JAMES PIATT,

Author of "Western Windows," "Poems of House and Home," etc.

CINCINNATI:

W. E. DIBBLE, PUBLISHER.

1881.

ELECTROTYPED AT
FRANKLIN TYPE FOUNDRY,
CINCINNATI.

TO

JOSEPH LONGWORTH.

BY PUTTING HIS NAME HERE, I GIVE TO MY BOOK,

NOT TO HIM,

A GIFT OF GRACE.

PREFACE.

THE following pieces, designed to express somewhat of life, character and sentiment in the region indicated by the title, or to describe Western landscape, have been so kindly received by critics and readers both at home and abroad, on their appearance in the author's previous volumes, that he has been encouraged to hope their presentation in one body might prove acceptable. The poems have been revised for this volume, and a few corrections have been made.

NORTH BEND, OHIO, *Oct.*, 1880.

CONTENTS.

IDYLS AND LYRICS, Etc.

CONTENTS.

IDYLS AND LYRICS

OF

THE OHIO VALLEY.

THE PIONEER'S CHIMNEY.

WE leave the highway here a little space—
(So much of life is near so much of death:)
The chimney of a dwelling still is seen,
A little mound of ruin, overgrown
With lithe, long grasses and domestic weeds,
Among the apple-trees (the ancestors
Of yonder orchard fruited from their boughs)—
The apple-trees that, when the place was rough
With the wild forests, and the land was new,
He planted: one, departed long ago,

But still a presence unforgotten here,
Who blessed me in my boyhood, with his hands
That seemed like one's anointed. Gentle, strong
And warmed with sunny goodness, warming all,
Was he, familiar by the reverent name
Of Uncle Gardner in our neighborhood:
His love had grown to common property
By those quick ties that Nature subtly knits,
And so at last had claimed the bond of blood.

He was an elder in the land, and held
His first proprietary right, it seemed,
From Nature's self; for, in an earlier day,
He came, with others who of old had reached
Their neighbor hands across New England farms,
Over the mountains to this Western Land, —
A journey long and slow and perilous,
With many hardships and the homesick look

Of wife and children backward; chose his farm,
Builded his house, and cleared, by hard degrees,
Acres that soon were meadows deep and broad,
Or wheat-fields rocking in the summer heat.

His children grew, and son and daughter passed
Into the world that grew around, and some
Into that world which, evermore unseen,
Is still about us; and the graveyard where
Their bodies slept (a few half-sinking stones,—
A stranger's eyes would hardly see them,—show
Seventy rods yonder in the higher ground)
Gave still a tenderer title, year by year,
To the dear places earned by earlier toil.

Meanwhile the years that made these woody vales
An eager commonwealth of crowding men
Passed, one by one, and every thing was changed;

And he, whose limbs were like the hickory's when
He came with life's wrought vigor here, was changed:
He heard the voice that tells men they are old.
Yet not the less he moved his usual rounds,
Walked his old paths; not idle, sweated still
With scythe or sickle in the hay or wheat;
Followed his plow, when, in the April sun,
The blackbird chattered after, and the crow
Far-off looked anxious for the new-dropped corn;
And gave the winter hours their services
With sheep abroad on slopes that, slanting south,
Breathed off the snow and showed a warming green,
With cattle penned at home, or bounding flail:
Thus—not forgetting social offices
Throughout all seasons, (gaining so the love
That went acknowledged in his common name,)—
He, like the Servant in the Parable,
Doing his duty, waited for his Lord. . . . .

The chimney shows enough for memory,
And, it may be, a traveler passing close,
If thoughtful, well might think a tender thought
Of vanished fireside faces, in his dream
Suddenly lighted by a vanished fire;
And should the apple trees that linger, loth
To end their blossoming, attract his eye,
Their fragrance would not pass unrecognized
For deeper gifts than fragrance. He is gone
Who planted them, and thirty years are gone.
Now, if you look a quarter-mile away,
Beyond the toll-gate and its lifted sweep,
You see a prouder house, not new nor old,
Beneath whose later roof no spirit dwells
That had its tenure here: a stranger holds
The secondary ownership of law.

It is a story, common though it seem,

Tender and having pathos for the heart
Which knows, but will not know, that he who says
"My own," and looks to-day on willing fields,
And sets his family tree in trusted ground,
To-morrow hears another answer "Mine."
Listen, if you will listen. It is hard
To go an alien from familiar doors
When we are young, to wrestle where we go,
And win or lose quick-hearted — we are strong;
But it is pitiful when weak and old,
When only for the near in life we seek,
And Heaven, yearned after, is not thought afar,
To lose our shelter and to want for rest.

Of Uncle Gardner's children three were dead;
Yonder they lie. Their mother and two with him—
Two youngest: one a boy of fourteen years
His latest child; a girl of seventeen —

Breathed in his still, contented atmosphere.
An elder daughter, wedded years before,
Lived far away in watery Michigan.
His eldest son, and the first-born of all,
Thrived as a merchant in the city near,—
Had thriven, at least, or so 't was said; and he
For some shrewd scheme had won the old man's will
To be his bond. The father pledged the land—
Willing for the grown man, yet for the boy
And for his girl at home reluctantly,
Holding the chance a rash one. From that day
He wrought his daily labors ill-content,
And with a trouble in his countenance.
To things familiar came a subtle change.
The brook that long ago, companion-like,
Had grown acquainted with his solitude,
And, later, made him music when he walked
And led his children through the pasture-ground

Up to the haying or the harvest gap,
A noisy mimic of their prattled words,
Now seemed to lift a stranger's face at him,
Wondering why he came there, who he was,
Or murmured, with a long and low lament,
Some undercurrent of an exile's song
That is not on his lips but in his heart.
Nothing was as it had been: something vague,
That Present of the Future which is born
Within the bosom, whispering what will be,
Met him and followed him, and would not cease
To meet and follow him: it seemed to say
"The place that knew you shall know you no more."
And oftentimes he saw the highway stirred
With slowly-journeying dust, and, passing slow,
The many who forever in our land
Were going farther, driven by goads unseen,
Or not content and looking for the new;

And then he thought of how in those dear days
He, too, had ventured, and again he saw
With steadfast eyes forgotten faces, known
When he was young, and others dear to him
From whom he parted with regret but firm
In the strong purposes which build the world;
Thought of his consolation — she most dear
Was with him, they most helpless with him, too,
For whom he sought a newer world of hope;
"But I am old," he murmured, "she is old,"
And saw his hand was shaken like his thought.

Such were his troubled fancies. When he slept,
In his slow dreams — with lagging team, the last
Of many that, in yonder meadows foaled,
Grew and became a portion of the place —
Journeying far away, and never more
Reaching his journey's goal, (a weary road

Whose end came only with the waking day,)
He seemed to pass, and always 't was the same:
Through new-built villages of joyous homes,
Homes not for him; by openings recent-made,
But not for him; by cultivated farms
Of other men—and always 't was the same.
Then, when he woke and found the dream a dream,
And through his window shone the sun and brought
The faint rich smell of the new-tasseled corn,
More fragrant from the dew that weighed it down,
He murmured of his fields—"For other men;
They are not mine. The mortgage will be closed;
The mortgage goes wherever I shall go."

So passed the quarter of a year, and so
The old man, burdened with his little world,
Felt it upon his shoulders, stooping down,
Bent more with this than every other year.

And summer passed to autumn: in his door
He sat and saw the leaves, his friends of old,
Audible in the sunshine, falling, falling,
With a continuous rustle — music fit
For his accompanying thought. At last it came,
The blow that reached his heart before it came,
For all was lost: the son, whose risk he placed
Both on his children's home and on his heart,
Was ruined, as the careless worldlings say —
Ruined indeed, it seemed, for on his brain
The quick stroke flashed: for many years the son
Breathed in a world in which he did not live.

The old man took the blow but did not fail —
Its weight had been before. The land was sold,
The mortgage closed. That winter, cold and long,
(Permitted by the hand that grasped his all,
That winter passed he here,) beside his fire

He talked of moving in the spring; he talked,
While the shrill sap cried in a troubled blaze,
Like one whose life was not all broken down,
Cheerfully garrulous, with words that show
False witnesses of hope and seeming strength
When these are gone and come not. In the spring,
When the first warmth was brooding every-where,
He sat beside his doorway in that warmth,
Watching the wagons on the highway pass,
With something of the memory of his dread
In the last autumn; and he fell asleep.
Perhaps within his sleep he seemed again
Journeying far away for evermore,
Leaving behind the homes of other men,
Seeking a newer home for those he loved,
A pioneer again. And so he slept——

And still he sleeps; his grave is one of those.

His wife soon joined his sleep beside him there.

Their children Time has taken and the world.

The chimney shows enough for memory,
The graves remain; all other trace is gone,
Except the apple-trees that linger, loth
To end their blossoming. In restless moods
I used to wander hither oftentimes,
And often tarried till the twilight came,
Touched with the melancholy wrought by change;
And something in the atmosphere, I thought,
Remained of hours and faces that had been.
Then, thinking of the Past and all I knew,
And all remembered, of it—most of him
Whose vanished fireside blazed so near me here—
My fancy, half unconscious, shaped the things
Which had been, and among the quiet trees

The chimney from its burial mound arose;
The ruined farm-house grew a quiet ghost—
Its walls were thrilled with fitful murmurs, made
Within by voices scarcely heard without;
And from the window breathed a vaporous light
Into the outer mist of vernal dark,
And lo! a crowd of sparks against the sky
Sprang suddenly, at times, and from the wood
(The wood?—no wood was here for forty years!)
Barked the shrill fox, and all the stars hung bright;—
Till, busy with the silence far away,
(And whether heard or heard not hardly known,)
First indistinct, then louder, nearer still,
And ever louder, grew a tremulous roar;
Then, sudden, flared a torch from out the night,
And, eastward half-a-mile, the shimmering train
Hurried across the darkness and the dream,
And all my fantasy was gone, at once—

The lighted window and the fireside sound:
I saw the heap of ruin underfoot,
And overhead the leaves were jarred awake,
Whispering a moment of the flying fright,
And far away the whistle, like a cry,
Shrill in the darkness reached the waiting town.

FIRE BEFORE SEED.*

HOW bright to-night lies all the Vale,
Where Autumn scattered harvest gold,
And, far off, hummed the bounding flail
When dark autumnal noons were cold!

The fields put on a mask of fire,
Forever changing, in the dark;—
Lo, yonder upland village spire
Flashes in air a crimson spark!

*It is customary in some parts of the West to rake the last year's stubble of corn into windrows in the Spring, and burn it, preparatory to breaking the ground for a new planting. This burning is generally done after night-fall:—its effect on the landscape these lines were intended to describe.

I see the farm-house roofs arise,
  Among their guardian elms asleep:
Redly the flame each window dyes,
  Through vines that chill and leafless creep.

Along the lonely lane, that goes
  Darkening beyond the dusky hill,
Amid the light the cattle doze
  And sings the awakened April rill.

The mill by rocks is shadowed o'er,
  But, overhead, the shimmering trees
Stand sentinels of the rocky shore
  And bud with fire against the breeze!

Afar the restless riffle shakes
  Arrows of splendor through the wood,
Then all its noisy water breaks
  Away in glimmering solitude.

Gaze down into the bottoms near,
  Where all the darkness broadly warms:
The priests who guard the fires appear
  Gigantic shadows, pigmy forms!

The enchanted Year shall here awake
  With harvest hope among her flowers;
And nights of holy dew shall make
  The morning smile for toiling hours.

Behold the Sower's sacrifice
  Upon the altars of the Spring!—
O dead Past, into flame arise:
  New seed into the earth we fling!

THE MOWER IN OHIO.

[JUNE, MDCCCLXIV.]

THE bees in the clover are making honey, and I
am making my hay:
The air is fresh, I seem to draw a young man's
breath to-day.

The bees and I are alone in the grass: the air is so
very still
I hear the dam, so loud, that shines beyond the
sullen mill.

Yes, the air is so still that I hear almost the sounds
I can not hear—

That, when no other sound is plain, ring in my empty
ear:

The chime of striking scythes, the fall of the heavy
swaths they sweep —
They ring about me, resting, when I waver half asleep;

So still, I am not sure if a cloud, low down, unseen
there be,
Or if something brings a rumor home of the cannon
so far from me:

Far away in Virginia, where Joseph and Grant, I know,
Will tell them what I meant when first I had my
mowers go!

Joseph, he is my eldest one, the only boy of my three
Whose shadow can darken my door again, and
lighten my heart for me.

Joseph, he is my eldest — how his scythe was striking
ahead!
William was better at shorter heats, but Jo in the
long-run led.

William, he was my youngest; John, between them,
I somehow see,
When my eyes are shut, with a little board at his
head in Tennessee.

But William came home one morning early, from
Gettysburg, last July,
(The mowing was over already, although the only
mower was I:)

William, my captain, came home for good to his
mother; and I'll be bound
We were proud and cried to see the flag that wrapt
his coffin around;

For a company from the town came up ten miles
with music and gun:
It seemed his country claimed him then—as well as
his mother—her son.

But Joseph is yonder with Grant to-day, a thousand
miles or near,
And only the bees are abroad at work with me in the
clover here.

Was it a murmur of thunder I heard that hummed
again in the air?
Yet, may be, the cannon are sounding now their
Onward to Richmond there.

But under the beech by the orchard, at noon, I sat
an hour it would seem—
It may be I slept a minute, too, or wavered into a
dream.

For I saw my boys, across the field, by the flashes
as they went,
Tramping a steady tramp as of old, with the strength
in their arms unspent;

Tramping a steady tramp, they moved like soldiers
that march to the beat
Of music that seems, a part of themselves, to rise
and fall with their feet;

Tramping a steady tramp, they came with flashes of
silver that shone,
Every step, from their scythes that rang as if they
needed the stone—

(The field is wide and heavy with grass)—and, com-
ing toward me, they beamed
With a shine of light in their faces at once, and—
surely I must have dreamed!

For I sat alone in the clover-field, the bees were
working ahead.
There were three in my vision—remember, old man:
and what if Joseph were dead!

But I hope that he and Grant (the flag above them
both, to boot,)
Will go into Richmond together, no matter which is
ahead or afoot!

Meantime, alone at the mowing here—an old man
somewhat gray—
I must stay at home as long as I can, making, myself,
the hay.

And so another round—the quail in the orchard
whistles blithe;—
But first I'll drink at the spring below, and whet
again my scythe.

READING THE MILESTONE.

I STOPPED to read the Milestone here,
A laggard school-boy, long ago;
I came not far — my home was near —
But ah, how far I longed to go!

Behold a number and a name, —
A finger, Westward, cut in stone:
The vision of a city came,
Across the dust and distance shown.

Around me lay the farms asleep
In hazes of autumnal air,
And sounds that quiet loves to keep
Were heard, and heard not, every-where.

I read the Milestone, day by day:
  I yearned to cross the barren bound,
To know the golden Far-away,
  To walk the new Enchanted Ground!

THE GRAVE OF ROSE.

I CAME to find her blithe and bright,
Breathing the household full of bloom,
Wreathing the fireside with delight;—
I found her in her tomb!

I came to find her gathering flowers—
Their fragrant souls, so pure and dear,
Haunting her face in lonely hours;—
Her single flower is here!

For, look: the gentle name that shows
Her love, her loveliness, and bloom,
(Her only epitaph a rose,)
Is growing on her tomb!

KING'S TAVERN.

FAR-OFF spires, a mist of silver, shimmer from
the far-off town;
Haunting here the dreary turnpike, stands the tavern,
crumbling down.

Half a mile before you pass it, half a mile when you
are gone,
Like a ghost it comes to meet you, ghost-like still it
follows on.

Never more the sign-board, swinging, flaunts its
gilded wonder there:
"Philip King"—a dazzled harvest shocked in West-
ern sunset air!

Never, as with nearer tinkle through the dust of
long ago
Creep the Pennsylvania wagons up the twilight —
white and slow.

With a low, monotonous thunder, yonder flies the
hurrying train —
Hark, the echoes in the quarry !— in the woodland
lost again !

Never more the friendly windows, red with warmth
and Christian light,
Breathe the traveler's benediction to his brethren
in the night.

Old in name, The Haunted Tavern holds the barren
rise alone ;—
Standing high in air deserted, ghost-like long itself
has grown.

Not a pane in any window — many a raggéd corner-bit:
Boys, the strolling exorcisors, gave the ghost their notice — "Quit."

Jamestown-weeds have close invaded, year by year, the bar-room door,
Where, within, in damp and silence gleams the lizard on the floor.

Through the roof the drear Novembers trickle down the midnight slow;
In the summer's warping sunshine green with moss the shingles grow.

Yet in Maying wind the locust, sifting sunny blossom, snows,
And the rose-vine still remembers some dear face that loved the rose, —

Climbing up a southern casement, looking in neglected air;
And, in golden honey-weather, careful bees are humming there.

In the frozen moon at midnight some have heard, when all was still—
Nothing, I know! A ghostly silence keeps the tavern on the hill!

FIRES IN ILLINOIS.

HOW bright this weird autumnal eve —
While the wild twilight clings around,
Clothing the grasses every-where,
With scarce a dream of sound!

The high horizon's northern line,
With many a silent-leaping spire,
Seems a dark shore — a sea of flame —
Quick, crawling waves of fire!

I stand in dusky solitude,
  October breathing low and chill,
And watch the far-off blaze that leaps
  At the wind's wayward will.

These boundless fields, behold, once more,
  Sea-like in vanished summers stir;
From vanished autumns comes the Fire—
  A lone, bright harvester!

I see wide terror lit before—
  Wild steeds, fierce herds of bison here
And, blown before the flying flames,
  The flying-footed deer!

Long trains (with shaken bells, that move
  Along red twilights sinking slow)
Whose wheels grew weary on their way
  Far westward, long ago:

Lone wagons bivouacked in the blaze,
  That, long ago, streamed wildly past;
Faces, from that bright solitude,
  In the hot gleam aghast!

A glare of faces like a dream,
  No history after or before,
Inside the horizon with the flames,
  The flames — nobody more!

That vision vanishes in me,
  Sudden and swift and fierce and bright;
Another gentler vision fills
  The solitude, to-night:

The horizon lightens every-where,
  The sunshine rocks on windy maize; —
Hark, every-where are busy men,
  And children at their plays!

Far church-spires twinkle at the sun,
  From villages of quiet born,
And, far and near, and every-where,
  Homes stand amid the corn.

No longer, driven by wind, the Fire
  Makes all the vast horizon glow,
But, numberless as the stars above,
  The windows shine below!

NEW GRASS.

ALONG the sultry city street,
Faint subtile breaths of fragrance meet
Me, wandering unaware
(In April warmth, while yet the sun
For Spring no constant place has won,)
By many a vacant square.

Whoever reads these lines has felt
That breath whose long-lost perfumes melt
The spirit — newly found
While the sweet, banished families
Of earth's forgotten sympathies
Rise from the sweating ground.

It is the subtile breath of grass;
And as I pause, or lingering pass,
With half-shut eyes, behold!
Bright from old baptisms of the dew,
Fresh meadows burst upon my view,
And new becomes the old!

Old longings (Pleasure kissing Pain),
Old visions visit me again—
Life's quiet deeps are stirred:
The fountain-heads of memory flow
Through channels dry so long ago,
With music long unheard.

I think of pastures, evermore
Greener than any hour before,
Where cattle wander slow,
Large-uddered in the sun, or chew

5

The cud content in shadows new,
Or, shadowy, homeward low.

I dream of prairies dear to me:
Afar in town I seem to see
Their widening miles arise,
Where, like the butterfly anear,
Far-off in sunny mist the deer,
That seems no larger, flies.

Thy rural lanes, Ohio, come
Back to me, grateful with the hum
Of every thing that stirs:
Dear places, saddened by the years,
Lost to my sight send sudden tears
Their secret messengers.

I think of paths a-swarm with wings
Of bird and bee — all lovely things

From sun or sunny clod;—
Of play-grounds where we children play,
And fear not Time will come to-day,
And feel the warming sod.

New grass: it grows by cottage doors,
In orchards hushed with bloom, by shores
Of streams that flow as green,
On hill-slopes white with tents or sheep,
And where the sacred mosses keep
The holy dead unseen.

It grows o'er distant graves I know:—
Sweet grass! above them greener grow,
And guard them tenderly!
My brother's, not three summers green;
My sister's—new made, only seen
Through far-off tears by me!

It grows on battle-fields — alas,
Old battle-fields in withered grass!
    New battles wait the new:
Hark, is it the living warmth I hear?—
The cannon far or bee anear?
    The bee and cannon too!

WASHINGTON, D. C., April, 1863.

THE BLACKBERRY FARM.

NATURE gives with freëst hands
Richest gifts to poorest lands.
When the lord has sown his last
And his field's to desert passed,
She begins to claim her own,
And — instead of harvests flown,
Sunburnt sheaves and golden ears
Sends her hardier pioneers:
Barbarous brambles, outlawed seeds,
The first families of weeds
Fearing neither sun nor wind,
With the flowers of their kind
(Outcasts of the garden-bound).

Colonize the expended ground,
Using (none her right gainsay)
Confiscations of decay: —
Thus she clothes the barren place,
Old disgrace, with newer grace.
Title-deeds, which cover lands
Ruled and reaped by buried hands,
She — disowning owners old,
Scorning their "to have and hold" —
Takes herself; the moldering fence
Hides with her munificence;
O'er the crumbled gatepost twines
Her proprietary vines;
On the doorstep of the house
Writes in moss "Anonymous,"
And, that beast and bird may see,
"This is Public property;"
To the bramble makes the sun

Bearer of profusion:
Blossom-odors breathe in June
Promise of her later boon,
And in August's brazen heat
Grows the prophecy complete;—
Lo, her largess glistens bright,
Blackness diamonded with light!
Then, behold, she welcomes all
To her annual festival:
"Mine the fruit but yours as well,"
Speaks the Mother Miracle;
"Rich and poor are welcome; come,
Make to-day millennium
In my garden of the sun:
Black and white to me are one.
This my freehold use content—
Here no landlord rides for rent;
I proclaim my jubilee,

In my Black Republic, free.
Come," she beckons; "enter, through
Gates of gossamer, doors of dew
(Lit with Summer's tropic fire),
My Liberia of the brier."

LAND IN CLOUD.

ABOVE the sunken sun the clouds are fired
With a dark splendor; the enchanted hour
Works momentary miracles in the sky;
Weird shadows take from fancy what they lack
For semblance, and I see a boundless plain,
A mist of sun and sheaves in boundless air,
Gigantic shapes of Reapers moving slow
In some new harvest:—so I can but dream
Of my great Land, that takes its Morning star
Out of the dusky Evening of the East:
My Land, that lifted into vision gleams
Misty and vast, a boundless plain afar,

(Like yonder fading fantasy of cloud,)
With shadowy Reapers moving, vague and slow,
In some wide harvest of the days to be —
A mist of sun and sheaves in boundless air!

A LOST GRAVEYARD.

NEAR by, a soundless road is seen, o'ergrown
with grass and brier;
Far off, the highway's signal flies — a hurrying dust
of fire.

But here, among forgotten graves, in June's delicious
breath,
I linger where the living loved to dream of lovely
death.

Worn letters, lit with heavenward thought, these
crumbled headstones wear;
Fresh flowers (old epitaphs of Love) are fragrant
here and there.

Years, years ago, these graves were made;—no mourners come to-day:
Their footsteps vanished, one by one, moving the other way.

Through the loud world they walk, or lie—like those here left at rest—
With two long-folded useless arms on each forgotten breast.

SUNDOWN.

WHILE fitful breezes kiss to frosty gold
The swells of foliage down the vale serène,
And all the sunset fills
The dreamland of the hills,
Now all the enchantment of October old
Feels a cold veil fall o'er its passing scene.

Low sounds of Autumn creep along the plains,
Through the wide stillness of the woodlands brown,
Where the weird waters hold
The melancholy gold;
The cattle, lingering slow through river lanes,
Brush yellowing vines that swing through elm-
trees down.

The forests, climbing up the northern air,
Wear far an azure slumber through the light,
Showing, in pictures strange,
The stealthy wand of change;
The corn shows languid breezes, here and there —
Faint-heard o'er all the bottoms wide and bright.

On many a silent circle slowly blown,
The hawk, in sun-flushed calm suspended high,
With careless trust of might
Slides wing-wide through the light, —
Now golden through the restless dazzle shown,
Now drooping down, now swinging up the sky.

Wind-worn along their sunburnt gables old,
The barns are full of all the Indian sun,
In golden quiet wrought
Like webs of dreamy thought,

And in their Winter shelter safely hold
  The green year's earnest promise harvest-won.

With evening bells that gather, low or loud,
  Some village, through the distance, poplar-bound,
      O'er meadows silent grown,
      And lanes with crisp leaves strown,
Lifts up one spire, aflame, against a cloud
  That slumbers eastward, slow and silver-crowned.

And form like the young hickory, so tough and
tall and lithe,
I first remember coming up — we came a wagon-
load,
A dozen for Old Hickory — this rough November
road.

Ah! forty years — they help a man, you see, in
getting gray;
They can not take the manly soul, that makes a
man, away!
It's forty years, or near: to-day I go to vote once
more;
Here, half a mile away, we see the crowd about the
door.

My boys, in Eighteen Sixty — what! my boys? my
men, I mean!

(No better men, no braver souls, in flesh-and-blood
are seen!)—
One twenty-six, one twenty-three, rode with their
father then:
The ballot-box remembers theirs — my vote I'll try
again!

The ballot-box remembers theirs, the country well
might know —
Though in a million only two for little seem to go;
But, somehow, when my ticket slipped I dreamed,
of Jackson's day:
The land, I thought, has need of one whose will
will find a way!

"*He* did not waver when the need had called for
steadfast thought, —
The word he spoke made plain the deed that lay
behind it wrought;"

And while I mused the Present fell, and, breathing
back the Past,
Again it seemed the hale young man his vote for
Jackson cast!

Thank God it was not lost! — my vote I did not
cast in vain!
I go alone to drop my vote, the glorious vote,
again;
Alone — where three together fell but one to-day
shall fall;
But though I go alone to-day, one voice shall speak
for all!

For when our men, awaking quick, from hearth and
threshold came,
Mine did not say, "Another day!" but started
like a flame;

And while I mused the Present fell, and, breathing
back the Past,
Again it seemed the hale young man his vote for
Jackson cast!

Thank God it was not lost!—my vote I did not
cast in vain!
I go alone to drop my vote, the glorious vote,
again;
Alone—where three together fell but one to-day
shall fall;
But though I go alone to-day, one voice shall speak
for all!

For when our men, awaking quick, from hearth and
threshold came,
Mine did not say, "Another day!" but started
like a flame;

I'll vote for them as well as me; they died as
soldiers can,
But in my vote their voices each shall claim the
right of man.

The elder left his wife and child — my vote for
these shall tell;
The younger's sweet-heart has a claim — I'll vote
for her as well!
Yes! for the myriad speechless tongues, the myriad
offered lives, —
Oh, desolation at the heart of orphans and of
wives!

I go to give my vote alone — I curse your shameless
shame
Who fight for traitors here at home in Peace's holy
name!

I go to give my vote alone, but, even while I do,
I vote for dead and living, all — the living dead and
you!

See yonder tree beside the field, caught in the sudden sough,
How conscious of its strength it leans, how straight
and steadfast now!
If Lincoln bends (for all, through him, my vote I
mean to cast) —
What winds have blown! what storms he's known!
the hickory's straight at last!

NOVEMBER, 1864.

THE DESERTED SMITHY.

AT the end of the lane and in sight of the mill
Is the smithy; I pass it to-day, in a dream
Of the days whose red blood in my bosom is warm,
While the real alone as the vanished I deem:
For the years they may crumble to dust in the heart,
But the roses will bloom though the grave-stones depart.

In the loneliest evenings of long ago,
The smithy was dear in the darkness to me,
When the clouds were all heaping the world with their snow,

And the wind shivered over dead leaves on the
tree;
Through the snow-shower it seemed to be bursting
aflame: —
How the sparks in the dark from the chimney came!

It was dear in the Past; and still it is dear,
In the memory fond of the far-away time,
When the binging and banging, and clinging and
clanging,
In the heart of my boyhood, were music and
rhyme;
When the bellows groaned to the furnace-glow,
And the lights through the chinks danced out in the
snow.

The irons within on the anvils were ringing:
There were glowing arms in the bursting gleam;

And shadows were glowering away in the gloaming,
  That, suddenly bounding to giants, would seem
Now out of the open doorways to spring,
Now up in the rafters vanishing!

The smith I remember: oh, many a smile
  Has played on his lips with me, and kind
Were the words that would lighten the dusk of his
    face—
  His face, at the memory, gleams in my mind—
With a heart that could beat in the heart of a boy,
A heart for his grief, and a heart for his joy!

Adown from the farm of my father once more,
  That so long has forgotten us up on the hill,—
With the wings in my blood to the bound of the
    steed,
  That passes the breezes so merry and shrill,—

I seem to be flying; then, suddenly, seem
To drop to the earth from the wings of my dream!

Vain dream of the Past!—But I pass it to-day:
  No longer the furnace is bursting with flame;
No longer the music comes out of the door,
  That, long ago, to the schoolboy came:
The winds whisper low through the window and door,
The chimney is part of the dust of the floor.

. . . Phœbe Morris! sweet Phœbe!—the sweetest
    of girls
  That brightened old dreams with a beautiful face!—
It may be that she smiled from her father's lips,
  And blossomed her smile in the dusky place!
Ah, she smiles, to-day, in my boyhood for me,
With her lips that are kissing—a memory!

GRANDFATHER WRIGHT.

HE knew of the great pioneering days,
And the dread Indian times that only live
In dreams of old men when the ember-ghost
Of long December evenings, Memory,
Rising from the white ashes of the hearth
And from the ashes of their outburnt lives,
Haunts them, and fills them with a tender breath
From the rough forests, full of wolves and deer,
Where their young hearts made the fierce land their own.

THE OLD MAN AND THE SPRING-LEAVES.

UNDERNEATH the beechen tree
All things fall in love with me!
Birds, that sing so sweetly, sung
Ne'er more sweet when I was young;
Some shy fay, (I *will* not see!)
Steals to kiss me, lovingly;
All the leaves, so blithe and bright,
Dancing sing in Maying light
Over me: "At last, at last,
He is stolen from the Past!"

Wherefore, leaves, so merrily mad?
I am rather sad than glad.

"He is the happy child that played
Underneath our beechen shade,
Years ago, — whom all things bright
Gladdened, glad with his delight!"

I am not the child that played
Underneath your beechen shade;
I am not the boy ye sung
Songs to, in lost fairy-tongue.
He read fairy dreams below:
Legends leaves and flowers must know;
He dreamed fairy dreams, while ye
Changed to fairies, in your glee
Dancing, singing, on the tree;
And, awakened, fairy-land

Circled childhood's magic wand!
Joy warmed his heart, joy kissed his brow;—
I am following funerals now.
Fairy shores from Time depart;
Lost horizons flush my heart.
I am not the child that played
Underneath your beechen shade.

"'Tis the merry child that played
Underneath our beechen shade,
Years ago,—whom all things bright
Gladdened, glad with his delight!"

Ah, the bright leaves will not know
That an old man dreams below!
No; they will not hear nor see,—
Clapping their hands at finding me,
Singing, dancing, on their tree!

Ah, their happy voices steal
Years away; — again I feel,
While they sing to me apart,
The lost child come in my heart:
In the enchantment of the Past,
The old man is the child at last!

THE LOST FARM.

THE SCHOOLMASTER'S STORY.

WHEN my strong fathers came into the West,
They chose a tract of land which seemed the best,
Near a swift river, in whose constant flow
Peacefully earth and heaven were one below;
Gigantic wardens, on the horizon, stood
Far-circling hills, rough to their tops with wood.

They came, a long and dangerous journey then,
Through paths that had not known of civil men;
With wives and children looking back, and still
Returning long in dreams confusing will,

They came, and in the panther-startled shade
The deep foundations of a State were laid.
The axe, in stalwart hands, with steadfast stroke,
The savage echoes of the forest woke,
And, one by one, breaking the world-old spell,
The hardy trees, long-crashing, with thunder fell.
The log-house rose, within the solitude,
And civilized the tenants of the wood.
It was not long before the shadow'd mold
Open'd to take the sunshine's gift of gold;
In the dark furrow dropp'd the trusted seed,
And the first harvest bless'd the sower's need.

Oh, dear the memory of their simpler wealth,
Whose hardship nursed the iron flower of health;
Oh, sweet the record of the lives they spent,
Whose breath was peace, whose benison content;
Unenvied now by us, their delicate sons,

The dangers which they braved, those heartier ones!
The Indian's midnight coming, long ago,
And the wolf's howl in nights that shone with snow,
These are but dreams to us (who would but dream),
Pictured far off, heard as lost sounds that seem:
They knew the terror, seventy years gone by,
Of the realities we may not try,
Who left the farm on which my new-born eyes
Saw the great miracle of earth and skies.

The fields were clear'd; the farm-house, girt around
With meadow-lands and orchards, held its ground;
The goodly place had wavering uplands, sweet
With cattle-pastures, hot with ripening wheat.
The house look'd Westward, where the river lay
Shimmering o'er level lands at close of day,
Or, many-twinkling through the autumnal morn,
In the hazy heat rustled the languid corn.

Not far were neighbors--heirs of acres wide,
Or the small farms in which the old divide.
By the close pike, a half-mile off to the north,
The tavern, with old-fashion'd sign thrust forth,
Show'd Washington, a little faded then,
(Too faded now, among new-famous men!)
And, close beside, the blacksmith-shop was found,
In August noons obtrusive with its sound,
Or late in winter eves, a welcome sight,
Burning and brightening through with bursting light!

Such was the farm—how dear to my regret!—
Whose fresh life runs into my bosom yet.
My dreams may bear me thither even now.
Again, with eager heart and sunburnt brow,
Homesick at times, I take a noiseless train,
Wandering, breath-like, to my home again;

See my glad brothers, in the June-sweet air,
Toss the green hay, the hot sheaves of harvest bear;
The fireside warms into my heart—how plain!
And my lost mother takes her boy again;
My sisters steal around me tenderly—
And all that can not be yet seems to be!

In thirty years what changes there have been!—
How disappear the landmarks that were seen!
If I should go to seek my boyhood's place,
What chart would show the way, what guide would
trace?

New people came. Around the tavern grew
New dwellings and new manners—all things new.
The impetus of something in the land
(Some gold, unseen, diviners understand),
Some mystic loadstone of the earth or air,

Drew all the nimble spirits of action there.
The village, not without a conscious pride,
Grew fast and gather'd in the country-side,
Then took the style of town. And now, behold,
A wild, strange rumor through the country roll'd !—
A railroad was projected, East and West,
Which would not slight us, so the shrewd ones guess'd.
Strange men with chain and compass came at last
Among the hills, across the valley pass'd ;
Through field and woodland, pasture, orchard, they
Turn'd not aside, but kept straight on their way.
Old farmers threaten'd, but it did no good—
The quick conservatives of the neighborhood.
"We do not want it !" many said, and one,
"Through field of mine I swear it shall not run !"
And paced his boundary-line with loaded gun.
Others replied (wise, weather-sighted, they !)

"You 'll think a little different, friend, some day.
The wheels of progress will you block—good speed!
(Cut off your nose to spite your face, indeed!)
'T will make the land worth double, where you walk."
"Stuff! stuff!" the old fogies answer'd—"how you
talk!"

The road was open'd. Soon another, down
Northward and Southward, cut across the town:
Both pass'd through meadows where my boyhood
stray'd:
One through the barn within whose mow I play'd.
And then a newer force of circumstance
Took hold and pull'd the place in quick advance:
The lovely river—swift, and deep, and strong—
Upon whose shore I fish'd and idled long,
(The still companion of my dreaming hour,)
Had great advantages of water-power.

Saw-mills and grist-mills, factories builded there,
Cover'd the banks and jarr'd the quiet air.
The river could not sleep nor dream its old
Beautiful dream, in morn or evening gold,
Or as a fallen soul had fitful glance
At its divine and lost inheritance.

The town became a city—growing still,
And growing ever, with a giant's will
Gathering and grasping, changing all it took.
A city sewer was my school-boy brook.
The farm remain'd, but only in the name;
The old associations lived the same.
The approaching city drew its arm around,
And threaten'd more and more the invaded ground;
Near and more near its noises humm'd and groan'd,
(Higher and higher priced the land we own'd!)
My father held his ground, and would not sell.

The stiff wiseacres praised his wisdom well.

At last I came from home. At college long
Absent, at home something, meanwhile, went wrong.
I need not tell the fact. What house is proof,
With jealous threshold and protected roof,
Against the subtle foes that every-where
Stand waiting to attack in safest air—
The insidious foes of Fortune or of Fate,
Who plan our ruin while we estimate
Our sum of new success? My father died—
(My mother soon was buried by his side;)
The farm pass'd into speculative hands,
Who turn'd to sudden profit all its lands.
The greedy city seized upon them fast,
And the dear home was swept into the Past.
Across its quiet meadows streets were laid,
White-hot, the dusty thoroughfares of trade.

Where the gray farm-house had its sacred hearth
Sprang buildings hiding heaven and crowding earth.

A score of years were pass'd. Return'd by chance
(A railway accident the circumstance)
To that strange city only known by name,
Unwilling visitor by night I came;
And, sleeping there within some great hotel,
There rose a dream that fills my heart to tell.
I came, a boy—it seem'd not long away—
Close to my father's house at shut of day.
I cross'd the pasture and the orchard where
Glimmer'd the cider-mill in golden air;
The faint, soft tremor of the wandering bell
Of cattle mingled with the old clover-smell.
I leap'd the brook that twinkled darkly bright,
And saw the farm-house dusk'd in mellow light.
The river, painted with the Western gleam,

Show'd through the leaves a Paradisal dream.
By the side-door my father met me then,
My mother kiss'd me in the porch again—
A moment all that was not was! I 'woke
And through my window saw the morning smoke
Of the loud city. And my dream, behold,
Was on the spot of the dear hearth of old!
A man's vain tears hung vague within my eyes.

The Lost Farm underneath the city lies.

THE FORGOTTEN WELL.

BY the old high road I find,
(The weeds their story tell,)
With fallen curb and fill'd with stones,
A long-forgotten well.

The chimney, crumbling near,
A mute historian stands,
Of human joy and human woe—
Far, faded fireside bands!

Here still the apple blows
Its bloom of rose-lit snow;
The rose-tree bless'd some gentle hands
With roses, long ago.

I can not choose but dream
  Of all thy good foredone ;—
Old alms-giver, thy gifts once more
  Show diamonds in the sun !

From yonder vanish'd home,
  Blithe children therein born ;
The mother with her crowing babe ;
  The grandsire palsy-worn ;

Strong men, whose weighted limbs
  Falter through dust and heat ;
Lithe youths in dreamland sowing deeds ;
  Shy maidens blushing sweet ;

The reaper from his sheaves ;
  The mower from his hay—

These take thy freshness in their hearts,
  And pass—my dream—away!

Forgotten by the throng,
  Uncared for and unknown,
None seek thee through the wood of weeds,
  Neglect has slowly sown.

Yet, under all, thou'rt there—
  Exhaustless, pure, and cold—
If but the sunshine came to see;
  The fountain ne'er grows old:

APPLE-GATHERING.

THE beautiful apples, so golden and mellow,
They will fall at a kiss of the breeze,
While it breathes through the foliage frosty and yellow
And the sunshine is filling the trees!
Though high in the light wind they gladly would linger
On the boughs where their blossoms were found,
Yet they drop at a breath, at the touch of a finger
They shatter their cores on the ground!

Through the morn of October while Autumn is trying
With all things to make-believe Spring,

How the leaves of the orchard around us are fly-
ing !—
The heavens with jubilee ring !
The ladders in breezes of sunshine are swinging,
The farmer-boys gladden and climb :
To gather the fruit they are swaying and sing-
ing—
Glad hearts to glad voices keep time !

Far down the bright air they are happy to listen
To the noise of the mill and the flail,
And the waters that laugh as they leap and they
glisten
From the dam that is lighting the vale !—
The wild flutter of bells that so dreamily rises
From glades where the cows wander slow,
And the laughter of faces in childish surprises
When the wind flings an apple below !

Oh, see! in the trees that are drinking the splendor,
  How the gladness of boyhood is seen!—
How they shake all the branches so windy and slender,
  And a quick golden rain is between!
High and higher they climb, till the grasses are cover'd
  With the fruits that were sweet April flowers,
And the yellowing leaves that all over them hover'd
  Flutter down with the apples in showers!

The harvests are garner'd, the meadows are burning,
  At sunset, in golden and brown;
The apples are gather'd, the wagons returning:
  The Winter may bluster and frown!
The blind-drifting snows may make barren the even,
  Dark twilights may shiver with rain;
But the apples and cider by Summer are given—
  Give Winter to Summer again!

FARTHER.

FAR-OFF a young State rises, full of might:
I paint its brave escutcheon. Near at hand
See the log cabin in the rough clearing stand;
A woman by its door, with steadfast sight,
Trustful, looks Westward, where, uplifted bright,
Some city's Apparition, weird and grand,
In dazzling quiet fronts the lonely land,
With vast and marvelous structures wrought of light,
Motionless on the burning cloud afar:—
The haunting vision of a time to be,
After the heroic age is ended here,
Built on the boundless, still horizon's bar
By the low sun, his gorgeous prophecy
Lighting the doorway of the pioneer!

TWO HARVESTS.

A MOUND IN THE PRAIRIES.

ALL day the reapers through the wheat
Have wrought amid the sultry heat,
Reaping the harvest wide and fleet.

All day the binders' stooping train
Have swelter'd through the sweating grain,
Binding the bearded sheaves amain :

With shouted jest, with breaks of song,
Lightening their heavy toil along,
A merry-hearted, boisterous throng!

But now, where all alone I stand,
The shocks like tents of gold expand,
The camp of Plenty in the Land!

Through the wide solitude around
Shrills but the empty dream of sound;
The Hours in golden sheaf lie bound.

Bathed in the crimsoning hush of air,
Yon mound, against the twilight bare
Breathes from a deeper twilight there.

The long grass rustled, year by year;
The herded bison thunder'd near;
Bounding in sunshine flew the deer.

The summers went, the summers came—
Years, years, years, years!—and all the same;
November's winding-sheet was flame!

The trees that hedge the prairies in
Have whispers dim of what has been,
Traditions of their crumbled kin.

Yon mound was still while centuries fled
And at their feet forgot their dead;
Nothing was ask'd and nothing said.

Now, vast with twilight's glamoury,
It whispers weirdly unto me;
Great dusky mirages I see.

In far-off days the Atlantic morn
Came not to find a world new-born;
Wide fields of sunshine shake with corn.

Lo, here an elder harvest land,
With many another reaper band!—
The tents of Plenty thickly stand.

All day the binders' stooping train,
Sweltering through the sweating grain,
Bind the hot-bearded sheaves amain:

With shouted jest, with breaks of song,
Lightening their heavy toil along,
A merry-hearted, boisterous throng!

And, as in those fair fields we see,
Through Bible-gates of memory,
In the high East shine beauteously:

Some Boaz owns the harvest plain,
Where, following the reapers' train,
See, Ruth, the gleaner, walks again!

Love, that had flush'd the centuries,
Lovely, as yonder, dwells with these;
And Faith, with nations at her knees!

The same sun shines, the same earth glows,
With the same transient joys and woes
The last man as the first man knows.

For Nature, swarthy mother, warms
(However changed their faces, forms,)
One human family in her arms!

The cattle low from field to fold;
The harvesters in evening gold
Leave the dusk shocks—the tale is told!

The silence falls, the twilight deep;
Myriads of morns the grasses creep
Across vast solitudes of sleep.

The herded bison thunder'd near;
Bounding in sunshine flew the deer;
The long grass rustled year by year.

Wolf, deer, and bison!—lo! the Wind,
A huntsman wild, to mad and blind,
Flinging his fiery torch behind!

MOORE'S CABIN.

I.

THE SHADOW-LAND.

ROUND us lies a Land of Shadow, not a footstep
echoes o'er;
Song of peace and cry of battle falter, dying, ever-
more.

War-fires in the vales are leaping, with the glaring
dance of war,
But the fiercely-gleaming faces are a painted dream
afar.

O'er the valley, clothed in shadow, sunlit stands the
startled deer,

From the cliff against the morning flashing away,
breath-like, with fear.

Lo, the golden light of morning o'er the Land of
Shadow cast,
Where the tomahawk is buried in the grave-mound
of the Past!

Nothing of that Land remains, now, save these gray
historic trees,
Shaking through their glittering branches dews of
olden memories!

II.

THE RUIN.

Here among the greenery hidden, warder of that
Shadow-Land,
Near the noisy-trampled highway, see the old dead
chimney stand!—

Hidden from the busy highway 'mong the cherries
large and low,
Whose new blossoms fill the breezes with a gentle
drift of snow!

Dead!—no more a flame is leaping through it toward
the wintry cold;
Dead!—no more its smoke is wreathing woodlands
deep and dim and old.

Dead!—no more its azure welcome gladdens eyes
that houseless roam;
Dead!—no more it seems uplifting incense from the
heart of Home!

Gone the hands that shook the forest, burying in the
furrow'd soil
Careful seeds of trust, returning harvest-guerdon for
their toil.

Gone the hearts that made pale faces, when the
wolves came starved with cold,
And the fireside still was waiting through the twilight snows of old.

Gone the homely cabin-threshold, with the feet that
cross'd it o'er;
Gone the closely-gather'd household, with their dwelling low and poor.

Yet I see a light of sparkles redden up old evenings
wild,
Like the fancies sent to wander up the chimney by
a child.

Hearts, I think, there may be, somewhere, echoing
through the vanish'd door,
Dreaming dreams returning, hearing footsteps from
the crumbled floor.

Children, whose new lives were darken'd here with
shades of sudden fears,
May be children, wandering hither, while old gray
men lose their years ;

They may hear the red-man's voices through the
night the silence start,
And, awaking, the old terror shiver newly through
the heart.

You may find them growing weary, faltering through
the busy lands,
Wrinkled by the years their faces, shaken by the
years their hands.

Of them here no token lingers, save the chimney
gray and low,
With a gleam of lighted faces from a fireside long
ago!

WALKING TO THE STATION

I WANDER down the woodland lane,
That to the turnpike greenly steals:
In breathless twilight gold, again,
To wait the far-approaching wheels;
To hear the driver's horn once more
Wind all around the river wood,
Shy echoes start along the shore
And thrill the bosky solitude.

Here, coming back last night, I 've found,
Of folk familiar once, how few!—
Some, blacken'd names in graveyard ground,
Forgotten on the farms they knew.

In our quick West the ruthless plow
  Spares not dear landmarks to displace;
The old Home, so long regretted, now
  Stared at me with a stranger's face!

Hark! the vague hum of wheels is blown,
  Fitful, across the evening calm—
No; 't is the far-off sound, well known
  To boyish ears, of Mower's dam.
I started later than I ought,
  It may be, and the stage is pass'd——
Fond fancy!—disenchanting thought,
  That will not let the fancy last!

Ah, broken dream! The wheels no more
  Ring faint beyond the Southern hill;
No longer down the valley roar,
  Waking the twilight bridges still;

No more the lonely farm it cheers
  To see the tavern's added light—
The stage is gone these seventeen years;
  I walk to meet the train to-night.

Yet here 's the crossing (ne'er a trace
  Of the old toll-gate toward the mill)—
The parting and the meeting place,
  Dear, dear to homesick memory still!
Oh, schoolboy-time of joy and woe,
  Of sad farewells, of blithe returns!—
I feel again the pang to go,
  The homeward rapture in me burns!

A sound grows busy with the breeze,
  A nearing roar, a glancing light,
A tremor through yon darkling trees—
  The fiery pant, the rushing might!

The head-light glares, the whistle screams;
  I cross the field, the platform gain.
Give back, for old regrets and dreams,
  Warm love and dear ones, flying train!

TRANSFIGURATION.

CRIMSONING the woodlands dumb and hoary,
Bleak with long November winds and rains,
Lo, at sunset, breathes a sudden glory,
Breaks a fire on all the western panes!

Eastward far I see the restless splendor
Shine through many a window-lattice bright;
Nearer all the farm-house gables render
Flame for flame, and melt in breathless light.

Many a mansion, many a cottage lowly,
Lost in radiance, palpitates the same
At the touch of Beauty strange and holy,
All transfigured in the evening flame.

Luminous, within, — a marvelous vision, —
  Things familiar half-unreal show;
In the effluence of Land Elysian,
  Every bosom feels a holier glow.

Faces lose, as at some wondrous portal,
  Earthly masks, and heavenly features wear;
Many a mother, like a saint immortal,
  Folds her child, a haloed angel fair!

OTHER POEMS.

THE GOLDEN HAND.

LO, from the city's heat and dust
A Golden Hand forever thrust,
Uplifting from a spire on high
A shining finger in the sky!

I see it when the morning brings
Fresh tides of life to living things,
And the great world awakes: behold,
That lifted Hand in morning gold!

I see it when the noontide beats
Pulses of fire in busy streets;
The dust flies in the flaming air:
Above, that quiet Hand is there.

I see it when the twilight clings
To the dark earth with hovering wings:
Flashing with the last fluttering ray,
That Golden Hand remembers day.

The midnight comes — the holy hour;
The city, like a giant flower,
Sleeps full of dew: that Hand, in light
Of moon and stars, how weirdly bright!

Below, in many a noisy street,
Are toiling hands and striving feet;
The weakest rise, the strongest fall:
That equal Hand is over all.

Below, in courts to guard the land,
Gold buys the tongue and binds the hand;
Dropping in God's great scales the gold,
That awful Hand, above, behold!

Below, the Sabbaths walk serene
With the great dust of days between;
Preachers within their pulpits stand:
See, over all, that heavenly Hand!

But the hot dust, in crowded air
Below, arises never there:—
O speech of one who can not speak!
O Sabbath-witness of the Week!

CINCINNATI, OHIO, 1859.

THE MORNING STREET.

ALONE I walk the Morning Street,
Filled with the silence vague and sweet:
All seems as strange, as still, as dead,
As if unnumbered years had fled,
Letting the noisy Babel lie
Breathless and dumb against the sky
The light wind walks with me, alone,
Where the hot day, flame-like, was blown;
Where the wheels roared, the dust was beat:—
The dew is in the Morning Street!

Where are the restless throngs that pour
Along this mighty corridor
While the noon shines?—the hurrying crowd
Whose footsteps make the city loud?—
The myriad faces, hearts that beat
No more in the deserted street?
Those footsteps, in their dreaming maze,
Cross thresholds of forgotten days;
Those faces brighten from the years
In rising suns long set in tears;
Those hearts—far in the Past they beat,
Unheard within the Morning Street!

Some city of the world's gray prime,
Lost in some desert far from Time,
Where noiseless ages, gliding through,
Have only sifted sand and dew,—
Yet a mysterious hand of man

Lying on all the haunted plan,
The passions of the human heart
Quickening the marble breast of Art,—
Were not more strange, to one who first
Upon its ghostly silence burst,
Than this vast quiet, where the tide
Of Life, upheaved on either side,
Hangs trembling, ready soon to beat
With human waves the Morning Street!

Ay, soon the glowing morning flood
Breaks through the charméd solitude:
This silent stone, to music won,
Shall murmur to the rising sun;
The busy place, in dust and heat,
Shall roar with wheels and swarm with feet;—
The Arachné-threads of Purpose stream,
Unseen, within the morning gleam;

The life shall move, the death be plain;
The bridal throng, the funeral train,
Together, face to face, shall meet
And pass, within the Morning Street!

1858.

THE END OF THE JOURNEY.*

OUR new-plucked flowers to the world's full
garland, friends!—
At home, with all best paths, his long Path ends.

Oh, such a Path no man e'er went before,
Earth-smiting king or patriot conqueror!

The sun's long path—the path it ever came
World-lighting—this his Pathway lit by fame.

Toward its own native East, the sun's great way
He went, with some new land each new-risen day.

*Written by request for the occasion of Gen. Grant's reception in Philadelphia, December 13, 1879, on the completion of his tour around the world.

At each land's threshold, as he crossed it, kings,
Warriors and statesmen gave him welcomings.

Crowned princes met him crownless, awed to see
In this still man the Great Land's majesty; —

O'er lands, o'er seas, they saw, through him confest,
The banded Stars that quicken all the West.

A hero's honors? — yes, a hero's, too:
But in the man the MANY-IN-ONE they knew.

The sun's long path — the path it ever came
World-lighting — this his Pathway lit by fame.

Toward the sun's native East, till the East was West,
And the sun rose across the roofs loved best!

—— Hark, with the cannon's thunder, "He is come,"
Mingle the martial trumpet, quickening drum, —

A warrior's welcome! . . . Let the war-sound cease;—
The warrior's welcome now be rest and peace.

The laurel, meed of mighty conqueror,
Long since we proudly gave, he justly wore.

Put up the sword, well-sheathed; upon the wall
The bow unstrung leave, wind-swayed, in the hall.

Long may he live, unvexed by clamorous cares,
Breathed on by blessing of health-breathing airs,—

Live long, grow old, like him our First of Men,
Or that plain Roman soldier-citizen.

Our new-plucked flowers to the world's full garland,
friends!—
At home, with all best paths, his long Path ends.

THE THREE WORK-DAYS.

SO much to do, so little done!
In sleepless eyes I saw the sun;
His beamless disk in darkness lay,
The dreadful ghost of YESTERDAY!

So little done, so much to do!
The morning shone on harvests new;
In eager light I wrought my way,
And breathed the spirit of TO-DAY!

So much to do, so little done!
The toil is past, the rest begun;
Though little done, and much to do,
TO-MORROW Earth and Heaven are new!

THE LOST GENIUS.

A GIANT came to me when I was young,
My instant will to ask—
My earthly Servant, from the earth he sprung
Eager for any task!

"What wilt thou, O my Master?" he began;
"Whatever can be," I.
"Say thy first wish—whate'er thou wilt I can,"
The Strong Slave made reply.

"Enter the earth and bring its riches forth,
For pearls explore the sea."
He brought, from East and West and South and North,
All treasures back to me!

"Build me a palace wherein I may dwell."
    "Awake and see it done,"
Spake his great voice at dawn. Oh, miracle
    That glitter'd in the sun!

"Find me the princess fit for my embrace,
    The vision of my breast;
For her search every clime and every race."
    My yearning arms were bless'd!

"Get me all knowledge." Sages with their lore,
    And poets with their songs,
Crowded my palace halls at every door,
    In still, obedient throngs!

"Now bring me wisdom." Long ago he went;
    (The cold task harder seems:)

He did not hasten with the last content—
The rest, meanwhile, were dreams!

Houseless and poor, on many a trackless road,
Without a guide, I found
A white-hair'd phantom, with the world his load
Bending him to the ground!

"I bring thee wisdom, Master." Is it he,
I marvel'd then, in sooth?
"Thy palace-builder, beauty-seeker, see!"
I saw the Ghost of Youth!

THE BOYS IN BLUE.

[TWO PROCESSIONS.]

GARFIELD, not only these do vote for you,—
Not only these, survivors tried and true,
Vote as they fought, the loyal Boys in Blue:

Not only these, who bore through shot and shell
The flag whose tatters keep their story well,
(New hands upraised it when the old bearers fell.)

Another mighty host comes marching slow
From their long bivouacs in the grass and snow—
By these they fought and suffered long ago.

Through every street they march with silent tread,
(Quicken the living, ye the Living Dead!)—
Look, the same tattered flag is overhead!

What captains lead them!—names well-kept as won.
(Lincoln looks down, the patient-featured one,
As erst I saw him, long years, in Washington:

He votes with them and these.) —The tried and true,
They vote; the dead, as living, vote for you,—
Vote, Garfield, as they fought, the Boys in Blue!

CINCINNATI, Saturday Night, Oct. 23, 1880.

CARPE DIEM.

TO-DAY I can not choose but share
The indolence of earth and air;
In dreamful languor lying,
I see, like thistle-flowers that sail
Adown some hazed autumnal vale,
The Hours to Lethé flying.

The hour-glass twinkles in the sun;
Unchanged its ceaseless course is run
Through ever-changeful weathers—
"*Time flies*," its motto: 't is no crime,
I think, to pluck the wings of Time,
And sleep upon his feathers!

A MAN'S VOTE.

[NOVEMBER, 1864.]

GO down into the ballot-box—from no uncon-
scious hand—
And, rising on the morrow morn, ring out through
all the Land!
Go down into the ballot-box, my single vote, to-
night:
Ring with a myriad, single-voiced, abroad in morn-
ing light!

Go down into the ballot-box, a righteous vote and
true—
No patriot's blood shall wasted seem, no bondman's
dream, for you!

Go down into the ballot-box, unheard, unfelt, unknown:
You shall be heard and felt and seen—the Day for you'll be shown!

If all the morn I held you fast, in silence and apart,
It matters not, O vote, you know I kept you in my heart!
Go down into the ballot-box—for Right at any cost;
And, what though last?—the polls are closed—thank God, you are not lost!

CONFLAGRATION.

I.

PLAYING with little children on the hearth,
    An hour ago—
    With fitful mirth
Their gentle eyes were lighted—lo! the Flame,
Like a lithe Fairy, to their fancies came,
    Whispering whispers low!

II.

All sleep. The harmless Fairy wakes and chases
Across the floor, and from the darkness crawls,
    Clambering up the walls,
And looks into the children's sleeping faces;
    Now through the window shines
    On the dew-burden'd vines;

CONFLAGRATION.

I.

PLAYING with little children on the hearth,
An hour ago—
With fitful mirth
Their gentle eyes were lighted—lo! the Flame,
Like a lithe Fairy, to their fancies came,
Whispering whispers low!

II.

All sleep. The harmless Fairy wakes and chases
Across the floor, and from the darkness crawls,
Clambering up the walls,
And looks into the children's sleeping faces;
Now through the window shines
On the dew-burden'd vines;

Then, Fiend-like, leaps,
Aloof,
Upon the roof!
The city sleeps.
It waves its myriad hands,
And laughs and dances, a maniac lost from bands!

III.

The scared bells ring!—
All sleepers, wakening, start
With fluttering heart!
Look! the gigantic Thing
The unimprison'd Fury, tosses high
Bloodiest arms against the frighten'd sky,
O'er streets that glare with men! Midnight gives way
To the flame-cradled day!
White Fear and red Confusion mingle cries:
"Arise! arise!

The city is in flame!"
The hearth-born Terror keeps its hurrying march,
The world aghast before, the clouds its victory-arch,
(The Larés on their altars die,
The wives and children fly :)
And ashes are its fame!

THE NEW HOUSE.

I.

THE BUILDING.

A STRANGER in the village street,
Shines the new house in morning light—
No quick enchantment sprung by night,
A vision for the sun, complete,
Like that the Arabian story shows:
For the slow toil of hours and days,
With steadfast hands and stalwart blows,
Wrought with the builder's brain, to raise
This temple, yet unconsecrate,
Of Home and Household Deities,
The stronghold of Domestic Peace,
Familiar Church and private State!

The builder he has watch'd it long,
Since first the pencil-plan was made
And the deep under-stone was laid,
The fast foundation firm and strong,
Through slow processes, day by day,
While floors were fix'd and rafters hung,
Till now—the workmen pass'd away—
He wakes from slumber, blithe and young:
Behold, at last, his work is done—
His house-in-air no longer dream,
Illumined by the morning gleam,
Transfigured by the rising sun!

II.

THE DWELLERS.

Come at Morning—you shall see
What a blissful company
Enter in the open door!

Children, children, evermore,
Dancing, singing, laughing, play,
Making merry holiday—
Happy faces, garments gay!—
Introducing Fairy-land,
Back to barren desert sand
Bringing flowers flown from earth;
The long coming-in of Birth!

Come at Midnight—you shall see
What a ghostly company
Pass from out the open door!
Old men, old men, evermore,
Wrinkled, dusty, travel-spent,
Burden-bearers bow'd and bent,
Songless, sighing, halting, slow,
In funereal garments go,
But, upon the threshold. lo!

Sudden children, vanish there,
Lost in light and lifting air,
Beautiful with blissful breath:
The long going-forth of Death!

TWO WATCHERS.

TWO ships sail on the ocean ;
Two watchers walk the shore :
One wrings wild hands and cries,
"Farewell for evermore."

One sees, with face uplifted,
(Soft homes of dream her eyes,)
Her sail, beyond the horizon,
Reflected in the skies !

[The above piece furnished Mr. George H. Boughton the suggestion for his beautiful picture, "The Two Farewells." The woodcut on the opposite page is made from the large steel engraving of that picture.]

PENCILLED FLY-LEAVES:

A BOOK OF ESSAYS IN TOWN AND COUNTRY.

BY JOHN JAMES PIATT.

1 *vol.* 16*mo.* $1.00.

Mr. Piatt has written a pleasant series of essays on a capital list of subjects. . . . It is the fashion with critics to make mention, more or less slightingly of detached pieces, bound up in book form. But, after all, how else should we have had Lamb and Hazlitt? . . Mr. Piatt is a poet, and sees the poetic side of everyday things. He is, besides, a genial optimist, and finds in the disagreeables of life—for instance, going to bed in a cold room—a delightful experience.—***Lippincott's Magazine.***

These essays are all infused with the same cheerful optimism, reflective spirit, sunny wisdom, and flavor of personal allusion which make the books of Hazlitt, Hunt, and Lamb, such delightful companions. Of Hunt, particularly, the writer often reminds us by his charm of manner, happy selection of theme, and not infrequent felicity of style.—***The (New York) Home Journal.***

Among the wit and humor and easy flow of pleasant things, pleasantly said, we have been most impressed with the essay on "Unexpected News of Death." Serious, without being somber, it sinks into the heart of the reader and carries him on in a stream of thoughtfulness which would not be unworthy of Lamb nor of Montaigne.—***The Independent.***

As might be inferred from the title, both grave and humorous elements are embraced in these essays. Pearls of thought and fancy are scattered through them all, and not a few of them are flavored with that quaintness and pathos which appeal both to the intellect and the best feelings of our common nature. No one but a person of true poetic sensibilities could write these essays. The author makes no parade of his mental culture, but he must be dull or blind who does not discover, on almost every page, in phrase, thought, image, or allusion, the flower and fruit of the writer's wide and sympathetic studies. Here are many passages and conceits that would have successfully appealed to the appreciation of Isak Walton, White of Selbourne, and Charles Lamb.—***The Western Christian Advocate.***

Mr. Piatt's style is perfectly simple; it would satisfy Wordsworth with its power of beautifying thought with common words. . . The elements of human life, the sources of affection, are made much of by Mr. Piatt, in his prose as in his poetry, so that life itself gains that value and importance which it is the province of literature as well as of religion, to give it, and which can be accomplished, as the result proves, without any straining after imaginative, romantic situation or dramatic effect.—***The Standard of the Cross.***

It is exquisite prose, too—pure, fresh, and sweet in every line. —***Cincinnati Commercial.***

For sale by all Booksellers. Sent, postpaid, on receipt of the price by the publishers.

ROBERT CLARKE & CO., CINCINNATI, O.

www.ingramcontent.com/pod-product-compliance
Lightning Source LLC
LaVergne TN
LVHW021409110826
845150LV00007B/1842

* 9 7 8 1 4 2 5 5 1 0 9 0 9 *